Mighty Machines
CARS

Ian Graham

QEB Publishing

This edition published for Scholastic Inc.,
557 Broadway; New York, NY 10012

Scholastic and associated logos are trademarks
and/or registered trademarks of Scholastic Inc.

Distributed by
Scholastic Canada; Markham, Ontario
Scholastic UK.; Coventry, Warwickshire

Published in the United States by
QEB Publishing, Inc.
23062 La Cadena Drive
Laguna Hills, CA 92653
www.qeb-publishing.com

Library of Congress Control Number: 2008010026

ISBN-10: 1-59566-133-6
ISBN-13: 978-1-59566-133-3

Printed in China

10 9 8 7 6 5 4 3 2

Author Ian Graham
Designers Phil and Traci Morash
Editor Paul Manning
Picture Researcher Claudia Tate

Publisher Steve Evans
Creative Director Zeta Davies

Words in **bold** can be
found in the glossary
on P. 23.

Contents

What is a car?

The job of a car is to carry us from place to place. Every car has an **engine**. The engine burns **fuel** and provides power to turn the wheels.

trunk

The trunk in the back of the car is for carrying things.

A car's engine is a complicated machine with hundreds of moving parts. Slippery oil keeps them all moving easily.

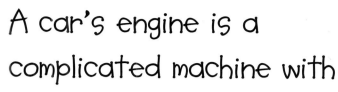

hood

In most cars, the engine is at the front, underneath the **hood**.

Everyday cars

Cars are made in all shapes and sizes. Small cars, or **compacts**, are good for short journeys. Business people who drive long distances prefer bigger cars with more powerful engines.

A car like this would suit a family with two small children.

4030 FHP

All cars need fuel.
The bigger the car,
the more fuel it uses.

To save fuel,
this **hybrid** car is
powered by electric
motors as well as a
gasoline engine.

Sports cars

Sports cars are designed to be fun to drive. They are small, lightweight, **maneuverable**—and fast!

Some sports cars have a top that can be folded down or taken off completely if the weather is nice. This type of car is called a convertible.

The low, smooth shape of this car helps it to go faster by letting air flow easily over it.

The Chevrolet Corvette has one of the biggest engines of any sports car.

Supercars

Supercars are the most powerful sports cars allowed on the roads. Some supercars have engines so big that they are like two ordinary car engines side by side!

air vent

This Ferrari Enzo has a top speed of 220 miles per hour (354 kilometers per hour). Vents at the front and side take in air to feed its massive engine.

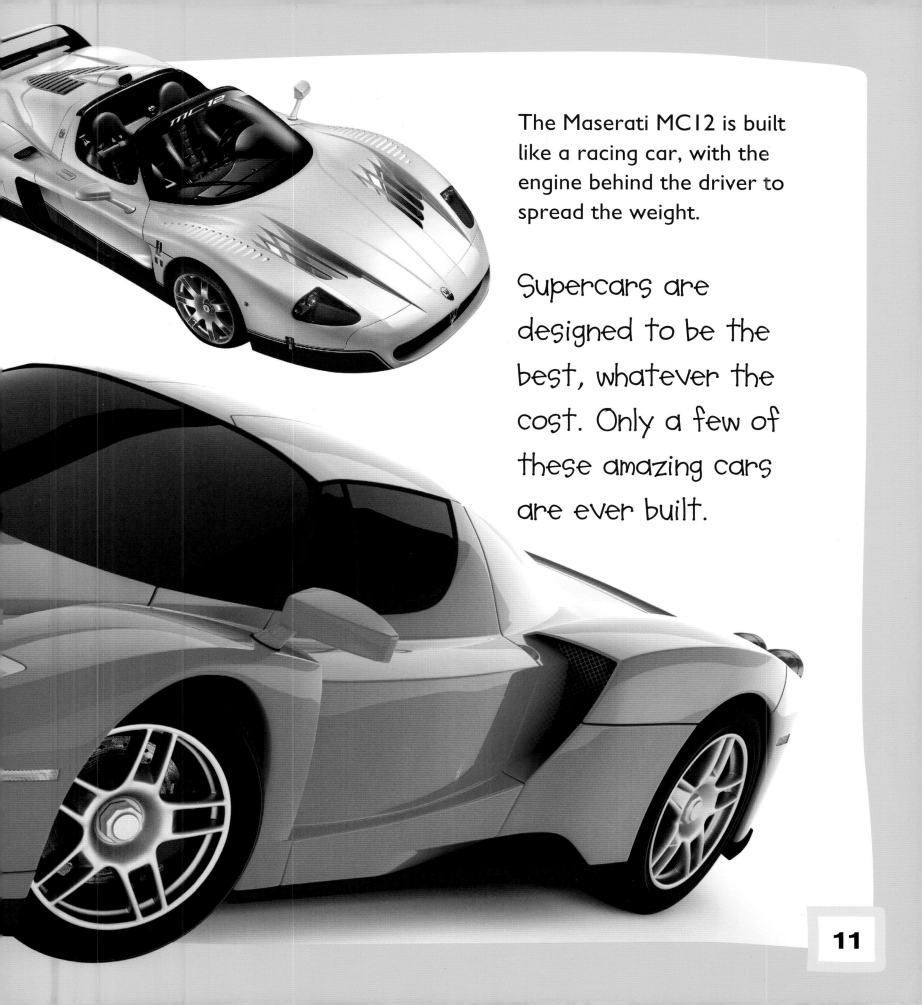

The Maserati MC12 is built like a racing car, with the engine behind the driver to spread the weight.

Supercars are designed to be the best, whatever the cost. Only a few of these amazing cars are ever built.

On the race track

Motor racing is one of the most **popular** and exciting sports. All sorts of cars can take part. There are races for sports cars, family cars, and specially built racing cars.

These NASCAR® cars are the same shape as ordinary cars, but each is a hand-built racer with a top speed of 200 miles per hour (322 kilometers per hour).

Top British driver Lewis Hamilton drives a Formula One racing car.

Formula One racing cars are all single-seaters. They are only half the weight of a family car but are 10 times more powerful—that's fast!

In the city

City cars that are used mostly for short journeys do not need to be big and powerful. In fact, the smaller they are, the better!

The Mini is small, but still has space for three **passengers**.

In towns and cities, smaller cars are a lot easier to park. They can squeeze into spaces where bigger cars will not fit.

This city car is so small that it can even park sideways.

Carrying more

People carriers, or MPVs (multi-purpose **vehicles**), have more space for passengers than ordinary cars.

The seats of an MPV are raised to give the driver and passengers a better view of the road. The back seats fold down easily to make extra carrying space.

This new MPV has seats that are very comfortable—like those in a movie theater.

This roomy MPV has eight seats and still has space for the groceries!

Going off-road

When the going gets tough, the car you need is an SUV (sport-utility vehicle).

With their chunky tires, SUVs can easily drive over rough or muddy ground without getting stuck. The engine also powers all four wheels to give more grip on mud, snow, and ice.

Only a **four-by-four** could plow through ground as wet and muddy as this!

This Hummer SUV is like the Humvee, the "go-anywhere" patrol car that U.S. Army soldiers drive.

chunky tires

Luxury cars

If you want to travel in real comfort, try a limousine! Limousines are mostly for important people, such as country leaders or celebrities. But they can be fun to hire for special occasions, such as weddings, too.

The president travels in this specially adapted Cadillac. The body is **armor-plated** and the windows are made of bulletproof glass for protection.

Rolls-Royce is a famous maker of luxury cars.

Extra-long luxury cars are called stretch limos. The longest stretch limos have five doors on each side and seats for up to 10 passengers!

Activities

- What kind of cars are these?

- Draw your own car and make up a story about it. What kind of car is it? Where is it going, and why? Who is traveling in it?

- Make a collection of pictures of different kinds of cars from magazines and comics. How many types can you find?

- If you had to drive along a muddy road, would a sports car or an SUV be better? Which car would you choose, and why?

- Which of these cars would be driven by a racing driver?

Glossary

Armor-plated
Specially strengthened to protect against bullets or missiles.

Compact
A type of car suitable for a small family.

Engine
The machine inside a car that provides power to make the wheels go round.

Four-by-four
A car in which the engine drives all four wheels, not just the two in the front or back.

Fuel
The liquid burned inside a car engine to make it go. Most car engines burn gasoline or diesel.

Hood
The part of a car's body at the front that protects the engine.

Hybrid
A car that saves fuel by using electric motors as well as a gasoline engine to drive the wheels.

Maneuverable
Easy to steer or control.

Passengers
The people who travel in a car along with the driver.

Popular
Liked by a lot of people.

Trunk
Space in the back of a car for carrying things.

Vehicle
A machine with an engine that carries people or things.

Index